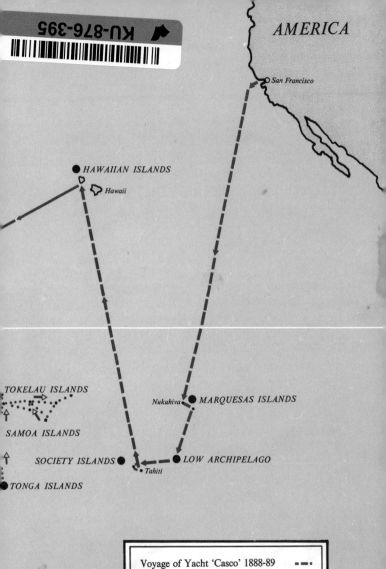

AMERICA

San Francisco

HAWAIIAN ISLANDS

Hawaii

TOKELAU ISLANDS

Nukuhiva ● MARQUESAS ISLANDS

SAMOA ISLANDS

SOCIETY ISLANDS ●

Tahiti

LOW ARCHIPELAGO

TONGA ISLANDS

W ZEALAND

Voyage of Yacht 'Casco' 1888-89	–·–·–
Voyage of Schooner 'Equator' 1889	———
Voyage of S.S. 'Janet Nicholl' 1890-91	····

ROBERT LOUIS STEVENSON

by BARBARA BRILL

with illustrations
by ROGER HALL

Ladybird Books Ltd Loughborough

ROBERT LOUIS STEVENSON

This is the story of a man who was born in Edinburgh, in Scotland and, though he ended his days in the warmth and sunshine of a South Sea island, he always thought longingly of his Scottish homeland. His native servants in Samoa, where he died, called him Tusitala, which means Teller of Tales, because he wrote stories. He was known throughout the world as Robert Louis Stevenson, the author of 'Treasure Island', 'Kidnapped' and many other books.

The story of Stevenson's life is as wonderful as the tales he told. It began at 8 Howard Place, Edinburgh, where he was born in 1850. His grandfather and his father were civil engineers specialising in work on rivers and harbours round the coasts of Scotland. They also built lighthouses, including that on the Bell Rock off the east coast of Scotland. This was the first lighthouse to be built on any site that was completely covered by the sea at high tide.

Stevenson's mother was delicate and, during the winter, her husband often took her away from Edinburgh to the warmer climate of the south of England or to France. Their only child, Robert—they always called him by his second name, Louis—was left in the care of his faithful nurse, Alison Cunningham. The little boy's name for her was 'Cummy'.

0 7214 0400 6

4

Like his mother, Louis was not very strong and suffered from coughs and colds. Much of his childhood was spent in his nursery with Cummy, where he played games of make-believe, with his toy soldiers and with a little model theatre. His cough often kept him awake at night, when Cummy would sit by his bed and tell him stories. He knew it was morning when they heard the carts begin to come into the city. In the daytime she looked at picture books with him and, when he was only three, taught him to recite poetry. They also played at being in church, when they would turn an armchair round to use as a pulpit.

Louis enjoyed looking out of the window in the evening to watch the lamplighter put up his ladder and light the lamp outside the house. Many years later Louis wrote a book of poetry for children called 'A Child's Garden of Verses' and included a poem about the lamplighter.

It starts like this:

My tea is nearly ready and the sun has left the sky,
It's time to take the window to see Leerie going by
For every night at tea-time and before you take your
    seat
With lantern and with ladder he comes posting up the
    street.

When he was six years of age, the family moved to Heriot Row nearer the centre of Edinburgh. A frequent visitor to this house was Louis' cousin Bob, who later became an artist. The boys painted scenes and figures for the toy theatre. For such plays as 'The Miller and his Men' and 'Three-fingered Jack', sheets of characters and views of ships, castles and forests could be bought at an Edinburgh shop. They were already coloured at twopence a sheet, or uncoloured, for a penny. The boys preferred the 'penny plains' and enjoyed daubing them with bright colours from their paint boxes.

Bob and Louis had other favourite games; they drew maps of imaginary kingdoms and pretended they were the rulers of kingdoms called Encyclopaedia and Nosingtonia and were at war with one another. Even their bowls of porridge were make-believe countries that became sprinkled with snow as they added their sugar, or were flooded with rain as they poured on the milk.

The cousins still remained close friends years later when Louis had become a famous writer and Bob a successful artist.

Louis had many other cousins whom he played with when he visited his mother's old home in Colinton, on the outskirts of Edinburgh. Here, his grandfather, Lewis Balfour, was the minister of the church. The old man lived in the manse (the vicarage) beside the church, with Louis' favourite aunt to look after him. It was a large house with stables and a coach house, and there was a garden sloping down to a mill stream where the children could play many games of 'let's pretend'. They would be Red Indians, hunters or soldiers and sometimes broke through the hedge to peer at the murky waters of the stream. They imagined that witches walked along the dark path beside the churchyard wall and that there was magic in the shadows cast by the lilac tree that stood in the centre of the lawn.

Louis loved the inside of the manse as much as the garden. His aunt was very kind and was always thinking of little treats to please him. When she bought him a box of tin soldiers, his grandfather taught him how to line them up for battle.

It was not all playtime for Louis however, for in spite of poor health he started school when he was seven. The school was near his home but he also had lessons from a visiting tutor whenever he was not well enough to leave his bed or to go out of the house. For one term, while his parents were abroad, he went to a boarding school. It was near London, where his aunt from Colinton was then living. He was not happy and wrote to his father:

"My dear papa, you told me to tell you whenever I was miserable. I do not feel well and I wish to get home. Do take me with you."

He went back to Edinburgh and started at another school, where he stayed until he was ready to go to the University. His father wanted him to study civil engineering and prepare to follow the family profession, but Louis had other ideas. He was a bright boy at school and did well in the subjects he enjoyed, particularly literature and Latin; he had already made up his mind that he wanted to be a writer one day.

His health improved and he became a ringleader in the pranks played by his school friends. He was now strong enough to join his parents on their travels abroad.

When he was thirteen he went with his father on a tour of inspection of the lighthouses round the coast of Fife. Four years later he began his studies for a science degree at Edinburgh University, and in the summer months when he was not studying, he still chose to be with his father's men at work on harbours and lighthouses.

Louis enjoyed his years at the University though he did not work as hard as he should have done. He made many friends whom his parents welcomed to the house. At this time he was still living at home, though as he grew older he increasingly wished to be independent.

His father leased a cottage as a holiday home. It was five miles from Edinburgh, at Swanston, by the foot of the Pentland Hills. Louis spent many vacations there either alone or with his friends. His cousin, Bob Stevenson, joined him when he came home from Cambridge and Louis was glad to be able to confide in him. He was now certain that he was not suited to engineering and instead wanted to be a writer. He was afraid of disappointing his father but surprisingly, Mr. Stevenson was sympathetic.

After some discussion it was decided that Louis should stay on at the University and study law so that he would have a profession to follow until he succeeded with his writing.

During his years as a law student, Louis began to write; wherever he went he carried a cheap notebook, scribbling down ideas and notes about people and things he noticed as he walked through the streets. His father did not approve of the time he spent in the shabby parts of Edinburgh, calling at inns and talking to the poorer people he met. His parents did not like the way he let his hair grow long, nor the loose-fitting velvet jacket and wide-brimmed hat he usually wore. They wished he would behave like the sons and daughters of their soberly respectable friends.

Louis was beginning to meet other writers and editors and all found him a gay companion whose conversation sparkled. A Cambridge professor, Sidney Colvin, recognised his talents as a writer and became his closest and lifelong friend.

The winter months in Edinburgh were trying ones for Louis, who still suffered from severe coughs and colds. When he was twenty-two he was so ill that the doctor insisted he went to the south of France where Colvin joined him. There his health improved and he became fit enough to go back to university and pass his final law examinations. His parents were very proud of him when the brass plate was put up outside the door to let everyone know that their son was a lawyer.

Stevenson did not spend much time in the law courts. His father made him a small allowance, and being free of his studies he began seriously to write and to travel. His essays and short stories were published in magazines and he completed his first book, 'An Inland Voyage'. It was about an unusual trip he made with a friend, travelling by canoe along the canals and rivers from Belgium to France.

Their canoes, the Arethusa and the Cigarette, caused quite a stir in the villages they passed through. On one occasion, after heavy rain, Louis' boat overturned in the flood water. He dragged himself up on to a tree that had fallen across the river, still clinging to his paddle, while the Arethusa floated rapidly away downstream until it was brought back by his friend.

They finally reached the attractive village of Grez, a favourite centre for artists on the river Loing. Louis had previously visited the village with Bob and he enjoyed the free and easy life there. During this visit he met a newcomer to Grez who was to change his life. This was Fanny Osbourne, an American lady, staying there with her daughter and son, Isobel and Lloyd.

Fanny came from California, and had married Sam Osbourne when she was only seventeen. She was now thirty-six and her marriage was breaking down. She had taken a trip to Europe with her children to get away from her husband and to study painting. Fanny and Louis were immediately attracted to each other, and he soon knew that she was the woman with whom he wanted to share his life. This was felt to be impossible while she was still married and Fanny began to consider the idea of a divorce.

His parents were shocked at the idea of Louis marrying a divorced woman, older than himself. His friends thought that he should be free to write and to travel, and not take on the responsibility of Fanny and her children.

Fanny returned to California to talk things over with Sam. Louis went away into the Cevennes mountains in France, to be alone with his thoughts, to walk and to write of his journey. He hired a donkey, Modestine, to carry his baggage, and with the animal as his only companion he walked through the mountains enjoying life in the open air, and sleeping in a tent. He wrote of his love of the outdoor life:

Give the jolly heaven above
   and the byway nigh me.
Bed in the bush with stars to see
Bread I dip in the river
There's the life for a man like me
There's the life for ever.

Against the advice of parents and friends, Stevenson was determined to follow Fanny to California. His father stopped his allowance, so for the first time Louis became dependent on the earnings from his writing. They were, as yet, barely sufficient to support him alone, quite apart from the additional burden of a family.

He had to travel as cheaply as possible, so he booked a passage on an emigrant ship sailing to New York. During the eleven-day voyage and in spite of cramped conditions on board, Louis spent many hours writing a short story and making notes for a book about the journey.

From New York he took a train to the Far West, an uncomfortable twelve-day journey that was a harsh experience for a man like Louis, who was by no means robust. Sometimes he sat out on the roof of the wagon looking out over the prairies.

He arrived in California feeling weak and ill; and during the next nine months his health steadily became worse. He tried camping for a while in the mountains south of Monterey and then went to San Francisco. There he lived in a workman's lodgings on very little money, writing hard all the time and sending his stories home to England for his friends to sell.

At last in the spring of 1880 Fanny was free to marry Louis. He was by then dangerously ill, and when news reached his parents of their son's state of health they sent a cable promising to send a regular allowance of money.

Fanny nursed him back to better health and in May they were married quietly in San Francisco. Then they took a trip northwards up into the mountains to Silverado where they hoped the air would help Louis to recover fully. By then, Fanny's daughter had married, but Lloyd, still a schoolboy, joined them on their honeymoon. Lloyd was very fond of his stepfather, whom he affectionately called Luly, and found him a wonderful companion, able to take a boyish delight in so many things.

Life at Silverado, a deserted silver mining camp, was a schoolboy's dream come true. They drove up the mountainside in a double buggy through the pine trees and found a tumbledown shack, once an office, with miners' bunk beds in the upstairs rooms. The view over the wooded hilltops to the distant valley was magnificent.

Fanny transformed the shack into a comfortable home. Louis rose early to do jobs like fetching water and chopping firewood. Then he wrote and rested in the peace of this quiet, lonely place. At last he grew strong again.

When Louis was fit to travel once more he, Fanny and Lloyd set out on a return journey to Scotland. He was eager to see his parents and for them to meet his wife. After a comfortable voyage, very different from the one Louis had made a year before, they landed at Liverpool and were met by his father and mother and Sidney Colvin.

Fanny had wondered how she would be received by Louis' parents. She had led such a different life from her respectable mother-in-law. Fanny was descended from Dutch settlers in America's mid-west and as a child had led a rough outdoor life. She had always been a tomboy and still wore her curly hair short and smoked cigarettes. With her dark skin and little, work-hardened hands that were used to cooking, gardening and sewing, she looked like a gipsy.

Her fears were needless. Louis' parents greeted her warmly and, seeing her devotion to Louis, thankfully accepted her as their daughter. They welcomed Lloyd too and enjoyed having a boy in the house once more.

After a few weeks in Edinburgh they all went up to the Highlands. Louis, seeing again the mountains, glens and lochs, found them more beautiful than ever.

As the winter drew near, Louis and Fanny made plans to go to Switzerland until the spring. He was sad to leave Scotland so soon for he had begun to take a keen interest in writing a book on Scottish history and was making notes in preparation. But the doctors knew that the Scottish winters were too damp and cold for him. They advised a stay of six months at Davos, a Swiss resort, where many people with lung weakness went to benefit from the mountain air.

Louis and Fanny left Scotland at the end of October taking Lloyd with them. They took, also, a new addition to the family, a black Skye terrier called Woggie, given to them as a wedding present by Louis' old canoeing companion. Living in a hotel among so many invalids, they were glad of the companionship of young Lloyd and Woggie, whom Louis took out daily for walks.

Louis found life very dull at Davos and felt hemmed in by the mountains. However, he enjoyed tobogganing and skating and he gradually became much fitter. But Fanny would not let him spend more than three hours writing each day. Throughout his life Fanny watched over him with care and never let him become overtired.

The following spring they came back to Scotland to a small cottage at Pitlochry which they rented for two months. Although it rained for days on end, Louis and Fanny were content to stay indoors and look out at the purple moorland and the mountains. They passed the time writing stories of ghosts and mysteries, that Louis called 'crawlers'. Among them were some of the best stories he ever wrote—'Thrawn Janet', 'The Merry Men' and 'The Body Snatchers'.

Later that summer they moved to Braemar but the weather was as bad as ever. One day Louis was watching Lloyd painting a map of an imaginary island that he had drawn. He joined the boy and began putting names on the map, such as Skeleton Island and Spyglass Hill. Then he wrote 'Treasure Island' in its top right hand corner and within five minutes jotted down a list of chapter headings under it.

By the next morning Louis had written the first three chapters for a story about this island, which was to be an adventure story for boys. He read it aloud to Lloyd, Fanny and his parents, and his father was as excited about it as Lloyd. Louis decided to go on and finish the story and to try to get it published. His choice for the title at first was 'The Sea Cook'.

Treasure Island

ye
Spye glass
Hill

Bulk of
Treasure
× here

○ Skeleton Isle

1. The Old Sea dog at the Admiral
Benbow
2. Black Dog appears and disapp
3. The Black Spot ○
4. The Chest The Sea Chest

The editor of a magazine called 'Young Folks' liked the opening chapters of 'The Sea Cook' and asked Stevenson to complete it for him as a serial story. Louis changed the title to 'Treasure Island'; later, in 1883, it was published as a book and was his first big success. He loved writing boys' books and wanted this to be the best book ever written about pirates. Lloyd was the first boy to hear the adventures of the one-legged sea cook, Long John Silver, and the boy hero, Jim Hawkins, who are now known all over the world.

Louis, Fanny and Lloyd went off to Davos again when the winter came. This time they stayed at a mountain chalet of their own where they were happier than in the hotel. The chalet had an attic which became a playroom for Lloyd. He and Louis staged battles there with toy soldiers on a large map drawn in chalk on the floor.

Sometimes they played with a toy theatre similar to the one of Louis' childhood. At other times they occupied themselves with a toy printing press. Louis carved woodcuts to illustrate short verses he wrote which Lloyd printed and made into little books.

After spending the summer again in Scotland the Stevensons did not go back to Davos. Tired of being always on the move, the following winter they found a house at Hyères on the French Riviera and stayed for over a year. Stevenson spoke of his days there as being some of the happiest of his life.

He was now successful with his writing. Readers in London and New York were beginning to know the initials R.L.S. He started a collection of verses for young children, to be dedicated to his nurse, Cummy, with a poem that included these lines:

> From the sick child, now well and old,
> Take, nurse, the little book you hold.

Just when it looked as though life would be more settled for Louis and Fanny, friends came to visit him and took him off with them to Nice. There he caught a severe chill. He was so ill that Fanny had to send for Cousin Bob to join them.

Louis recovered slowly but he had to spend many weeks in bed keeping as still as possible. Sometimes he was not allowed to speak a word. He hated the life of an invalid but he managed to sit up in bed and add new verses to his 'Child's Garden of Verses', as he called his collection.

Unfortunately, before Louis had fully recovered, an outbreak of cholera in Hyères forced them to leave. They went back to England, to Bournemouth, where Lloyd was now at boarding school. Old Mr. Stevenson bought a house there as a present for Fanny, of whom he had grown very fond.

Louis renamed the house 'Skerryvore' after a light-house built by an uncle off the rocky west coast of Scotland. The Skerryvore at Bournemouth was very different from its Scottish namesake. Within sight of the sea, it was a modern brick house covered with ivy. Seagulls skimmed over the lawn and doves fluttered into a large dovecote in the centre of the garden.

During the three years they spent at Bournemouth Louis led the quiet life of a semi-invalid, and travelled little. His friends came to visit him frequently and the house was always full of company.

In 1886 he had published another serial story for boys called 'Kidnapped', a tale of adventure in the Scottish highlands. Later he completed a book in as little as three days. This book was based on a dream he had about a doctor mixing a potion that could transform a good man into an evil man. He called it 'The Strange Case of Dr. Jekyll and Mr. Hyde' and it was an immediate success both in England and America.

In the winter of 1886 old Mr. and Mrs. Stevenson also took a house in Bournemouth. Louis' father was growing old and feeble and found comfort in the companionship of his son. He died early the following year and his death brought great changes to the family.

Louis and Fanny had stayed in England for the last three years to be within easy reach of the old man. Now they felt free to set off again in search of a place where Louis need not lead the life of an invalid and where old Mrs. Stevenson could join them. They decided to visit America, Fanny's homeland, and to look for a mountain resort.

Louis held a farewell party in London for his closest friends. They all expected to see him again within a year. Sidney Colvin saw them off on the 'Ludgate Hill', a ship being used as a cattle boat that carried a cargo of horses. Louis and his mother particularly enjoyed the voyage. She wrote in a letter:

"It is very amusing and like a circus to see the horses come aboard."

They stayed in New York, where Louis, well known as the author of 'Dr. Jekyll and Mr. Hyde' was now greeted as a celebrity. The party then went up to the Adirondack Mountains.

There they lived in a wooden house on the shores of Lake Saranac near a sanatorium for patients suffering from a lung complaint, as Louis was. Fanny went north to Canada to obtain a supply of furs which were badly needed in the bitterly cold weather that followed.

His enjoyment of the Atlantic voyage had made Louis eager to go to sea again. When Fanny made a journey to California to see her relations, he asked her to make enquiries in San Francisco about hiring a yacht for a sea cruise. Three months later Fanny sent him a telegram to say that the yacht Casco could be hired for a cruise among the islands of the South Seas. Louis telegraphed back to say that they would go. The money left to him by his father could pay for the voyage.

The Casco belonged to a Californian millionaire and was a lovely boat with tall masts, white sails, glittering brass and a luxurious saloon. The Casco's regular skipper, Captain Otis, was to be in charge with a crew of five including a Chinese cook.

In June, 1888, they went aboard and set sail. Their destination was the Marquesas Islands, 3,000 miles southward across the open sea.

Stevenson was overjoyed to be at sea again. He felt better than he had for years, no longer an invalid but a man of action like the heroes in his books. The sun shone and the sea was calm until they were halfway to the Marquesas. Then, without warning, clouds would blow up and suddenly the Casco would be caught in a squall with tropical rains pouring down and the sea pounding over the deck.

Louis and his mother were excellent sailors but Fanny suffered from seasickness. She endured the discomfort because of the obvious improvement she saw in her husband's health. She went about bare-foot, wearing loose-fitting clothes, and Louis needed only a singlet and trousers. Old Mrs. Stevenson however, still managed to look spick and span in the clothes she had worn in Edinburgh, complete with boots and a widow's cap. Most evenings they sat on deck and watched the sunset and the phosphorescence on the water with the coming of night.

After six weeks at sea, they saw at dawn the island of Nukuhiva. In his diary Louis noted how the isle lay shimmering before them as the sun rose. From that day he fell under the spell of the South Sea islands.

During the next two years the Stevensons visited many groups of islands in the Pacific. The Casco took them to Tahiti and Hawaii, then they boarded a trading schooner, The Equator, that took them to the Gilbert Islands and Samoa. Another trading schooner, The Janet Nicholl, took them on a four-month trip, during which they called at thirty-three islands.

After a year, old Mrs. Stevenson returned to Scotland but Louis and Fanny decided to delay going home because his health had so much improved in the South Seas. He was writing an account of his travels and had plans for a history of the Pacific islands.

They had fallen in love with the island of Samoa and decided to buy a plot of land there and build a house. At first it was to be merely a retreat to which he would return after a voyage home, but eventually they decided that they would make Samoa their permanent home. Louis wrote home to his friends:

"It would be hard to go back to England and to bed."

Their plot of land was over 300 acres on the side of Mount Vaea that rose up behind Samoa's chief port of Apia. Waterfalls and streams tumbled down the hillside so they gave it the Samoan name 'Vailima', meaning five streams.

At first Fanny and Louis camped out in a temporary wooden house as they had done at Silverado. They watched their permanent home taking shape on a plateau 600 feet above sea level. It had a large hall, lined with redwood panelling, occupying the whole of the ground floor. Outside, a veranda ran the full length of the house. There were five bedrooms and a library upstairs. Later, Louis had a study built on to the front of the house like a bird's nest above the veranda. Everyone went barefoot about the house and except for the sounds of the sea and the songs of the birds a deep silence reigned over Vailima. It was an ideal home for a writer.

Words flowed endlessly from Louis' pen. Throughout his travels, whether on sea or ashore, and whether sick or well, he had never stopped writing, completing stories, essays and poetry and jotting down ideas and notes for new books. Settled in his island home he wrote more eagerly than ever and even found time for regular letters to his friends.

Often his thoughts turned with longing to Scotland and he imagined that he was back in his homeland as he wrote of the Highlands in 'Catriona' and of Swanston in 'St. Ives'.

Louis spent regular hours writing and the rest of the day he enjoyed the happy and bustling life of the Vailima household. His mother had returned from Scotland, Lloyd was still with them and his sister, Isobel, her husband and son joined them.

Fanny took enormous pleasure in growing crops and cultivating the garden. To help her she had a team of faithful native servants who joined in the daily family prayers that were held in the great hall. The prayers were led by Louis, who wrote many of them himself.

Their furniture from Skerryvore was shipped out and when they entertained, the table in the hall was spread with linen and shone with silver and glass. A bust of Louis' grandfather looked down on the scene.

At first there was only a rough track up to Vailima, but the natives laid a broad road and called it the Road of Loving Hearts. The Samoans were devoted to their Tusitala—the Teller of Tales.

Louis hid his homesickness for Scotland except in his letters to his friends and in his poems. In one he wrote:

"Be it granted to me to behold thee again in dying,
Hills of home! and to hear again the call,
Hear above the graves of the martyrs the peewees
   crying
And hear no more at all."

In 1894, Louis began working on a novel about Scotland, 'Weir of Hermiston'. One evening in December, after spending most of the day on the ninth chapter, he came down to talk to Fanny and to play cards. He said he would make a salad for their meal and went to fetch a bottle of wine. As he came back he suddenly put his hands to his head exclaiming, "What's that? Do I look strange?" and fell on his knees beside Fanny. She helped him to an armchair and he lay there unconscious.

When the doctor came he said that Louis had a clot of blood on the brain and that there was no hope. He died the following day, December 3rd, aged just forty-four. The next day they buried him on the summit of Mount Vaea. Scores of natives worked through the night to clear a way to the mountain top and dug a grave, 1,300 feet above sea level. The grief of his family and friends was deep and heartfelt.

Eventually a large tomb was built over his grave. On the side were carved the words of a poem he had written fifteen years before, when he little imagined that he would sail the South Seas and be buried on a Samoan hillside. It includes these lines:

> "Here he lies where he longed to be
> Home is the sailor home from sea
> And the hunter home from the hill".